Horse Racing Terms

AN ILLUSTRATED GUIDE

Rosemary Coates

MERLIN UNWIN BOOKS

First published in Great Britain by Merlin Unwin Books Ltd, 2018

Text © Rosemary Coates 2018
Illustrations © Rosemary Coates 2018

Merlin Unwin Books Ltd
Palmers House
7 Corve Street
Ludlow
Shropshire SY8 1DB
UK

www.merlinunwin.co.uk

ISBN 978-1-910723-74-6

Typeset in Times by Merlin Unwin Books

Printed by 1010 Printing International Ltd

With special for their editorial assistance to Cheryl Needham,
John Pearn, Phil Lodge, Kay Gardner and Adrian McGlynn.

Foreword

Periodically, promoters of horse racing protest that its peculiar jargon is arcane and impenetrable. *"What is a furlong, a handicap, a gelding?"* they query. *"How can we engage with a new audience if we persist with this ancient language?"*

Thankfully, the sport resists this piffle. It is never the language that is wrong, merely the education. At heart, the sport is breathtakingly simple. A herd of exquisite equines racing each other, with the one whose brown – sometimes grey – nose crosses the finishing line first being the winner. It's been that way for centuries. But behind that simplicity, as with so many glorious endeavours, lies fascinating complexity.

Clarifying it is the purpose of this fabulous work by Rosemary Coates. Unpicking the sport's jargon with pithy freshness, and illustrated to great comic effect, this book will quickly enable anyone to acquire, with impressive fluency, the language of the Turf – the language of the world's greatest sport.

Adrian McGlynn, Director, Weatherbys

For a full alphabetical list
of racing terms – *see* page 137.

Gone to Post

'Gone to post' is when the horses and jockeys canter to the start before a race. That canter down is watched by punters to see how well the horse is moving. In the early days of racing, the start was a marker post. Today for Flat racing the start is from the stalls and for National Hunt, the Starter has elastic tape stretched across the track which he releases when the horses are lined up behind the tape. Goodwood and Salisbury have tape starts for their long distance races.

The Gate

A term sometimes used to describe the starting stalls used to start Flat races.

Jump or 'National Hunt' races are started by an elastic tape stretched across the track for the horses to line up behind and which is released at the same time as the Starter drops his flag to start the race.

In addition, the gate is the number of people who attend a race meeting.

Trainers

The trainer is the person in overall charge of the horse's training or the headmaster.

Lady trainers were not allowed to hold a licence in their own name until 1966 when Florence Nagle challenged the Jockey Club in the High Court and won. There are some very successful lady trainers today, especially in National Hunt racing.

Permit to Train

A Permit Holder can train horses to run 'under Rules'. He or she can only train horses for immediate family members: himself/wife/civil partner/his parents or grandparents/sons and daughters/ grandchildren/his brothers and sisters/ or a person who appears to be cohabiting with the holder of the permit by reason of a personal relationship and includes any Administrators of any of the above.

A Permit Holder cannot train horses to run on the flat (except for bumpers – *see* page 105) or horses owned by individual members of the public.

A Public Trainer can do all of these things.

String

A 'string' is the
collective noun for the
number of racehorses
a trainer has in his stable
be it Flat racing
or jump racing.

Stable Lads / Lasses

These are the working staff who look after the horses, they range in age from teenagers to more mature people. Each person has a certain number of horses to look after – can be up to about four – and they muck them out, groom them, and exercise them.

Head Lad

Oversees the lads/lasses and the horses on behalf of the trainer. In fact he is responsible for running the yard containing the horses. The travelling Head Lad is in charge of getting the horse to the races and is responsible for all the equipment/tack once at the races.

Maiden Stakes

They are for horses who have never won a race.
Some maidens may have finished in the top three
or four places and have won considerable 'place'
prize money but never *won* a race in their careers.

A maiden horse can be either sex. When it eventually finishes first, it has 'broken its maiden'. Maidens can be either Flat or National Hunt or Point-to-Point races.

A Good Trip

A horse that has had a 'good trip' did not experience unforeseen difficulties. A 'bad trip' might involve getting boxed in by other horses. When a horse has the stamina for a long race of, say, three miles or four miles, then in National Hunt terms the horse is said to 'get the trip' or 'stay the trip'.

The Classics

These races are the crème de la crème of the Flat racing season. Geldings cannot run in the English classics.

The top Flat races are: **1000 Guineas** run at Newmarket (fillies only, first run in 1814) **2000 Guineas**, also Newmarket (colts, first run in 1809) **The Oaks**, at Epsom (fillies, first run in 1779)

The Derby, Epsom (3-year-old colts and fillies, first run in 1780). **The Irish Derby** at the Curragh, Co. Kildare. **The St Leger** (both sexes, 3-year-olds) at Doncaster first run in 1776).

Fillies can run in both colts classics but rarely do so. In 1844 the Derby was won by a 4-year-old running under an assumed name. He was later disqualified.

Punter

Someone who bets on the horses.

Gambling on horses was certainly going on in Roman times when everyone took bets on the racing charioteers. Punters can bet on or off course, online, with a bookmaker or on the Tote.

Not everyone at a race meeting gambles. A few just enjoy watching the horses race, or having a good social time of it.

Biggest gambling fixtures of the year include the The Derby, The Grand National, The Cheltenham Festival and Royal Ascot.

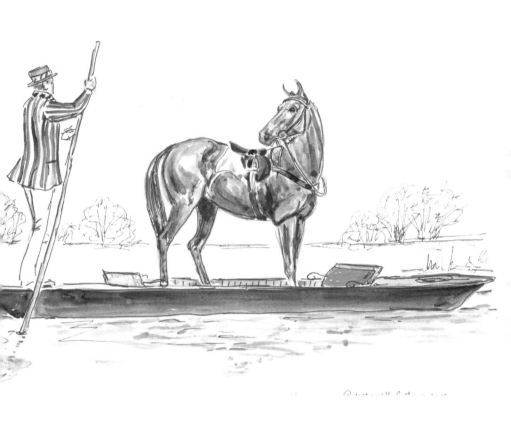

Turf Accountant

A rather upmarket name for a bookmaker or bookie. The collective noun for bookies at the races is the 'Ring' and they can be found 'On the Rails'.

Harry Ogden was perhaps the first UK bookmaker in the 1790s and The Gaming Act 1845 allowed betting at racecourses. But the big change came in 1961 when High Street betting shops were legalised.

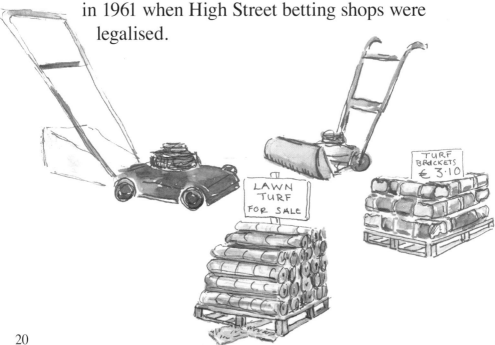

LAWN TURF FOR SALE

TURF BRACKETS €3·10

Bar

If commentator or bookmaker offers odds on the rest of the field at '10-1 bar' this means they are at longer odds than that.

Racing Double

A bet on two horses to come in first in two separate races.

Treble – for three horses to win in three separate races.

Forecast – a bet on two horses in the same race to come first and second.

Tricast (or Trifecta) – a bet on three horses in the same race to come first, second and third in a specified order. A Combination Tricast is when the three horses chosen need only finish in the first three but in any order.

Yankee

This gives you 11 bets as follows: 6 doubles, 4 trebles and 1 four-fold accumulator. You make four selections and at least 2 must be correct to get a payout. Perhaps not a bet for beginners.

Canadian
or **Super Yankee**

A wager involving 10 doubles, 10 trebles, 5 four-folds and one accumulator and one five-horse accumulator. A total of 26 bets.

A Pony

A £25 bet on a horse to win a race. Thought to have been brought back by soldiers from India where 25 rupee notes had a picture of a pony on them. Back in the UK 25 rupees morphed into £25, in betting terms a pony.

A Monkey

£500 bet. It is a similar story to that of a 'pony' (opposite), only the 500 rupee note had a picture of a monkey and this was translated to a £500 bet – a monkey.

A Banker

A horse expected by its connections (Trainer, Owner, Stable) to win.

On the Nose

A bet for a horse to come first in a race.

Alternatively, in a tight finish a horse can be said to have **won by a nose**.

Each-Way Bet

An 'each-way' or 'both ways' bet is on the horse
to win and/or be placed. A £10 each-way bet will
cost you £20. In handicap races of more than 16
runners, a 4th place qualifies as a place and will

pay out. In races with 8-16 runners, an each-way
bet pays out only on 1st, 2nd and 3rd place. In
races with between 5-7 runners only the first two
pay out. If 4 or fewer horses run, a win only pays.

On the Nod

Horses' heads go up and down when they run and a horse may win if his head is down and the rival's head is up.

The photo-finish camera was introduced in the UK 1947 to show which horse's head was first on the line as they crossed.

On rare occasions a finish has been declared a dead heat. Backers of both horses win money but at half the odds they would have received if their horse had won outright.

Pony-ed

In America the horses are led down to the starting post by a rider mounted on a pony or small horse. This is known as being 'pony-ed.

In Europe the horses and jockeys canter down to the start without being led. Occasionally, a horse will go down to the start earlier before the others to keep it calm.

Weighing Room

Before every race, the jockey is 'weighed out', and he is 'weighed in' when he returns at the finish of the race. This anxious moment is supervised by the Clerk of the Scales.

The weigh-in is important because the horse must return carrying the same weight the jockey weighed out in. He must weigh in within a certain time after the race is completed with the correct weight or he will be disqualified. Which is particularly galling if the horse had won or been placed.

The official Handicapper, who has been appointed by the British Horse Racing Authority (BHA) allocates the weights a horse must carry. This will affect the speed at which he can gallop. The official Handicapper and his team cover all racing, both Flat and National Hunt.

Scratched

This is when a horse is withdrawn from a race, either before the next entry stage or declaration stage.

Withdrawn at the start is when a horse has spread a plate (shoe) on the way to the start and cannot be re-shod, or refuses to go into the stalls and is withdrawn by the Starter, sometimes described as 'withdrawn not under orders'. If this happens, punters have their original stake returned to them on conclusion of the race.

Non-runner: If a horse is declared to run but due to illness or injury the trainer wishes to withdraw it, a vet's certificate may be required. If a self-certificate is used, the horse may not run for the next 7 days.

A trainer can make his/her horse a non-runner without penalty on account of the ground, if there has being a change in the going since the day of declaration.

39

Winning Distances

A win is a win, but it can be by a Nose, a Short head, Head, Neck, half a length, three-quarters of a length, a length, several lengths and a distance, which is when a horse wins by an enormous margin.

(*see* **Judge** page 84, **Camera** page 32, 85 and **On the Nod** page 33).

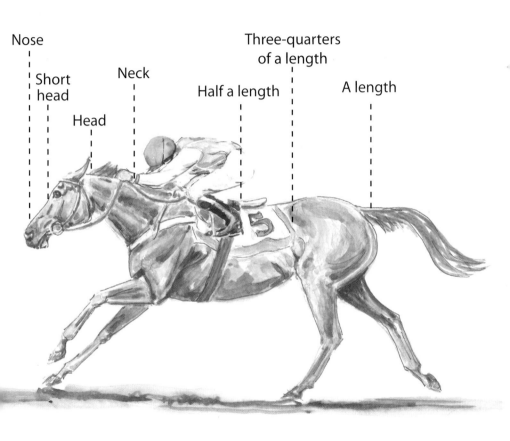

Nose

Short head

Head

Neck

Half a length

Three-quarters of a length

A length

Stall Handlers

They help all horses to load into the starting stalls and are used only in Flat racing. They are especially good when a horse is reluctant to enter the stalls.

The horses must be loaded quickly and efficiently in order for the race to start on time.

Each race meeting requires at least 11 fully-trained and BHA-accredited stall handlers. The number is increased for fields of over 20 horses.

The Draw

48 hours before a Flat race, or 24 hours before
jumps, the competing horses must be 'declared'
to run. When those declarations are processed,
a computer program randomly allocates a stall

number to each horse. A few prestigious handicap races such as the Stewards' Cup at Goodwood have a manual draw and the trainer can choose the stall. This can be important in a short race or if the track has better ground on one side.

Starter

The man in charge of starting the race at the designated time. Horses are 'under starter's orders' when he lifts the flag which he then drops as he presses the starter button that opens the stalls (Flat race) or releases the tape (National Hunt).

Sometimes the Starter may be a retired jockey who has retrained. They also need to know which horses they might have a problem with at the start.

The Assistant Starter inspects each horse's tack and in particular the girth which may need to be tightened. He also stands well behind the lined-up horses to crack a whip as the tape is released and the race starts.

Assistant Starter

All racecourses have an Assistant Starter who
at the start of a National Hunt race stands well
behind the horses and cracks a whip when the flag
goes down. (He does not hit the horses with the
whip!)

He is also the one who checks the girths etc
at the start and if it is a Flat race makes sure the
right horses go into the correctly numbered stalls
with the help of the stall handlers.

The Assistant Starter would be paid and trained
by the British Horseracing Authority.

Schooling

The term used to teach horses to race. Trainers will say 'the horse schooled over fences/hurdles this morning and he went very well'.

The Trainer is the equivalent of the head teacher i.e. he or she is the person in charge. He will also have an Assistant Trainer and the Head Lad all of whom report back to him.

He may train horses for several different owners or syndicates or exclusively for a single individual i.e. for J. P. McManus or a huge thoroughbred racehorse ownership, training and breeding operation such as Godolphin in Newmarket, Suffolk, which is one of the most famous racing establishments in the world.

Jockeys

An **Apprentice jockey** is someone under the age of 23, attached to a trainer for no less than three years in Flat racing who has not won more than 95 races. In National Hunt racing he/she is known as a Conditional jockey.

A **Conditional jockey** is an apprentice National Hunt racing jockey in Great Britain or Ireland under the age of 26 who has not won more than 75 races under rules.

Flat apprentices also claim weight off – *see* 'Riding out a claim' page 139.

A **Professional jockey** races for a living. Many jockeys are freelance and employ an agent to get them rides.

A **Stable jockey** is retained by a trainer or owner.

Lady or female jockey can be a professional or an amateur. Women were not allowed to hold a licence in the UK and Ireland until 1972 and could not compete as professional jockeys until 1976. Women were allowed to compete with men in the USA in 1968, in Australia in 1979 and in NZ in 1977. An **Amateur jockey** rides unpaid. Only amateurs can race at Point-to-Points, and some even make it to the big National Hunt races, such as the Grand National, and Cheltenham.

Jockey Club

This was the original governing body regulating racing and received its Royal Charter in 1750. Today it is the largest commercial group in British horse racing, in charge of racing estates and racecourses.

It manages 15 leading racecourses, the National Stud and the charity Racing Welfare. It has invested over £415 million pounds in horse racing in the UK.

In July 2007 the British Horseracing Authority (BHA) was formed both to govern and regulate the sport.

This freed The Jockey Club to focus on investing in and generating returns from its commercial interests, to plough back into the sport.

Turf Club

The Irish governing body for horse racing. The Irish Jockey Club originally met at the Rose and Bottle Inn and called themselves the Society of Sportsmen.

In 1784 it changed its name to the Turf Club.

The Turf Club was the regulatory body for all horse racing in Eire and Northern Ireland until 31st December 2017 when the Turf Club's name changed to the Irish Horse Racing Board.

Flat Racing

These are the races with no jumps and they call for a different type of horse to the jumping horses. Although still thoroughbreds, the Flat horses are usually the same height but will have a slighter build to the National Hunt horses: they are built for speed but not jumping strength.

The English Flat racing season starts just after the Grand National held at Aintree, and during the summer and winter months there is Flat racing on the 'All weather' courses.

Flat Jockeys ride in Flat races and Jump Jockeys over the fences (National Hunt). A horse can run on the flat if its trainer has a Dual Licence i.e. a Public Licence, whilst a Permit holder may only train horses to go over the jumps.

The only 'Flat' races a Permit holder may run his horses in is the National Hunt Flat race known as a 'bumper' (*see* page 105).

Jockey's Retainer

No, not a jockey's manservant but the fee to retain the services of a jockey who will then give first call to that particular trainer or owner.

However, he may accept 'outside' rides in races in which he is not riding for the owner or trainer who has 'retained' him.

Valet

The Valet is the person who looks after the jockeys and their equipment in the Changing Room and on the racecourse.

Each race they make sure the jockey has the right 'colours' or 'silks' and the correct riding weight to allow the jockey to weigh out with his saddle and weight cloth.

Some retired jockeys become valets.

Turf

The grass racing track is the norm in the UK, Ireland and most of Europe. There are some Flat turf tracks in America and US jump races are all on turf.

The turf is subject to the weather, which affects the 'Going' so the turf is officially inspected and declared by the Clerk of the Course, to be either Heavy, Soft, Good or Firm. There may be an inspection on the day of racing eg. in the case of frost, and the racing may be declared 'off'. Or there can be a second inspection a little later that morning and if conditions have improved then racing is 'on'.

Stallion, stud

A male horse who has retired to stud and is used for breeding. Often referred to as an 'entire'.

After a successful career on the race track the 'entire' horse or stallion is retired to stud, where, if things go well, he'll make more money for his connections than he did on the racecourse.

A successful racehorse will be much sought-after and the stud can be picky about the mares that are sent to him. The better the breeding and performance of the dam (mare), the better the progeny, one hopes.

In his first year he will cover about 120 mares, increasing to about 200, unless he is much sought-after and has a second breeding season in the Southern Hemisphere, in which case his number could be as much as 400 or more, flying back and forth twice a year.

After four years the stallion's first crop of foals will be starting to race. If these prove to be indifferent the stud's popularity will plummet and with that, the stud fees. Fees that were worth thousands can drop to just a few hundred pounds, euros or dollars.

Shuttle Stallion

This is one who, after he has finished his stud duties in the Northern Hemisphere, is flown for the breeding season in the Southern Hemisphere which doubles the number of mares he can cover in a year. (AI is not used in thoroughbred racehorse breeding)

Before flying the horses have to go into quarantine for two weeks before travelling. This is to make sure they are not carrying any notifiable disease.

On arrival at their destination they will spend a further two weeks in quarantine before being released to their respective studs. They travel two to a crate (known as stalls) and these are lifted into the plane. Experienced grooms travel with them, and sometimes a vet.

Brood Mare

A brood mare is a female horse who is selected for breeding (known as retiring to the paddocks) because of her own breeding and because she has won a significant number of good races. Listed races and Graded races are known as 'black type' races which show as such in her racing achievements.

The breeding season starts in February and goes on until June. This is because a foal is a year old on 1st January after he is born, even if foaled on 31st December.

The gestation period is 11 months. The mares may get artificial light to bring them in to season early so they are mated early in the year to give their foals a greater time in which to grow before racing.

Foals

Are youngsters in their first year. In the northern
hemisphere they become yearlings on their first
birthday which is on 1st January – even if they are
born on 31st December! Horses are yearlings in
their first year, then 2-year-olds upwards, and after
it is 10 years old it becomes 'aged'.

They are raced in the appropriate race for their age on the Flat, starting at 2 years old. For National Hunt the horses do not start racing before they are 3 years old.

A male foal is a colt until he is 4 when he becomes a horse, entire or stallion, unless he becomes a 'Bachelor Uncle', ie. he has been gelded (known as the cruellest cut of all!)

A female foal is a filly until she is 4 when she becomes a mare. She becomes a broodmare when she starts having foals when she has been retired to the paddocks.

Facial Markings

Horses can have very distinct head markings. The more common ones include:

Stripe: a narrow white mark down the face.

Blaze: a broad white stripe down the face which extends over the nose.

Star: white mark on the forehead.

Snip: white mark between or over the nostrils.

White face: includes the forehead, eyes and part of the muzzle.

If your horse has large white blaze, the racing commentator might be heard to say 'and the big white face of... is approaching the leaders.'

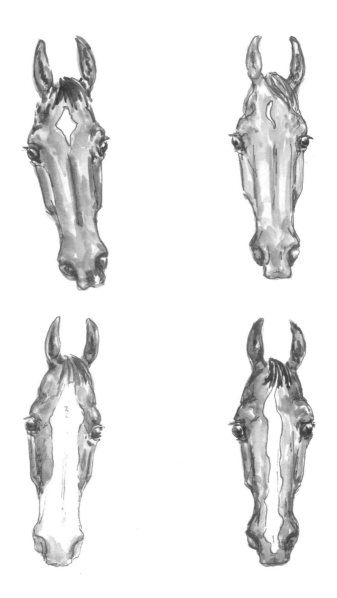

Colours

The colour of the 'points' is the deciding factor in determining the colour of a horse. Points are the mane, tail and the extremities (to the knee) of all four legs.

Horse colours include:

Black – black in colour with black points

Brown – dark brown or nearly black with brown points

Grey – even if it is white

Chestnut – ginger or a reddish colour with similar coloured mane and tail. **Light, dark** and **liver chestnut** are variations.

Bay – brown-coloured horse with black mane, tail and often black legs to the knee

'Green Horse' – a horse which is young and inexperienced

'Dark Horse' – one of any colour whose form is unknown!

Legs

1. 'Extra leg' is when a horse saves itself from falling on landing badly after a jump. The commentator on the race might say a horse has found an extra leg.

2. 'Own a leg' – syndicate members often claim to 'own a leg' of a racehorse, meaning that they are part of a consortium which shares the costs and rewards of jointly putting a racehorse into training and racing it.

3. 'Has a leg' can mean a bad leg injury – 'broken down' is a tendon problem and means the horse may or may not come back to racing after a long lay-off to allow it to heal.

4. 'Change a leg' means that the horse has changed its gait to lead with the other leg in a gallop.

Hands

Horses are measured in 'hands'. A 'hand' is 4 inches which was thought to be the width of a human hand. This measurement was standardised in 1541 by King Henry VIII.

Racehorses are usually 15.2 hh and upwards: occasionally you might find in National Hunt or Flat racing a horse that is under 15.2 hh which despite its lack of inches is still very successful.

A 15.2 hh racehorse would be considered small, 16–16.2 hh normal for both Flat and National Hunt racing, while 17hh and over is not unusual in National Hunt racing.

Hands are measured
from withers to floor

4
INCHES

Socks

'Socks' are white leg markings below the knee. 'Stockings' are markings that go above the knee. It is rare for a thoroughbred racehorse to have stockings.

A small band of white around the coronet –
where the hoof meets the leg hair of the coat – is
known as a coronet.

Runners

A runner is a horse which has been entered to compete in a race. When it has been walked with the other runners in the race around the parade ring and mounted by the jockey it goes down to the start and 'comes under starters orders'.

A 'runner' is also a person employed by a bookie to lay off any excess commissions by transferring them to other bookmakers (presumably saving his legs with a computer these days!)

Officials

Clerk of the Course is licensed by the British Horseracing Authority and is in overall charge of the racecourse. He is responsible for the running of the racecourse and sees that the strict rules of racing are upheld.

Stewards are appointed by the British Horseracing Authority. Each panel includes two Stipendiary Stewards. They watch the races for any infringement of the rules.

They are empowered to call a '**Stewards' Enquiry**' at which the two jockeys concerned will give evidence. They are empowered to impose fines and suspensions for over use of the whip, or for causing obstruction to any other horse and thus depriving it of its chance of winning the race.

The Judge He has a special box where he can view the whole race (he must be present in the judge's box for the duration of every race or it will

be declared void) and he sees the order in which
the horses pass the winning post. He is assisted
with the camera. An announcement will go out for
a 'Photo' in a close finish.

Veterinary Officer

He or she is appointed by the governing body of horse racing to oversee the regulatory aspects – drug-testing and scanning microchips etc.

All racehorses in the UK and Ireland must be drug-free which means that they must cease taking medication for any ailment at least 14 days before a race so that there is no trace of any medicine in their system. This also ensures that a horse runs in peak condition.

The Veterinary Officer also assesses the horse's condition or determines whether it is lame and therefore cannot be raced.

Veterinary Surgeon

Usually a local vet engaged by the racecourse to attend to the horses' welfare and medical needs on the day. Cheltenham employs 20 such vets for the Gold Cup Festival.

Bridles

Nosebands in sheepskin help the horse to concentrate on looking forward, while sheepskin cheek pieces distract a horse from worrying about what's behind.

Bridle with plain noseband

Blinkers are partial hoods to prevent a horse from seeing behind or to the side. These are used to sharpen up a horse.

Hood

Visors are similar to blinkers except there is a lateral slit in the eye covering so the horse can discern what's coming from behind. Blinkers and visors must be presented to the Clerk of the Scales before they weigh out.

Sheepskin noseband

Sheepskin cheek pieces

Visor

Blinkers: often in a hood these days

Hoods can include blinkers or visors. Some have ear coverings to minimise the noise of the racecourse for the horse. The hoods are weighed along with the jockey and saddle etc before a race. Once a horse has been declared by its trainer to be wearing a certain piece of equipment it *must* run in it.

Owners

They come from all sorts of backgrounds. There are the traditional owner/breeders, some of whose families have been involved since racing began. There are the big racing owner/breeding businesses.

Some people own just one horse, perhaps from a farming family, while others part-own horses with family and friends.

There are racing clubs, groups who invest in several horses for an annual fee. There are the big racing owner/breeding businesses such as Coolmore, Godolphin, Juddmonte.

There are some pubs and clubs/syndicates which have just one horse.

Also Ran

Term used for the rest of the field (the other horses in the race) that finish, but not in the top placings (ie. they didn't come first, second, third or fourth).

Rings

The punter at the racecourse can choose how much he or she wants to pay be there. The public enclosures are known as rings, usually only at the larger race meetings. Smaller racecourses only have a Members' Enclosure which usually consists of an internal area with a bar. Those with annual membership have metal enamelled badges. A day member payment can also be made. Perks here usually include a more salubrious bar and restaurant. There is Tattersalls ring which is next to the Members'. The Silver ring is so-called because many years ago, there was still change (silver) from a £1 when paying the entrance fee.

From all areas there is access to the parade ring (the paddock), the area around which the horses entered for a particular race, parade in front of their owners and trainers and where the trainers give instructions to their jockey before they mount the horse and leave the parade ring to go onto the course and down to the start.

Bookmakers have their stands in all the rings, and the Tote is also accessible to everyone.

Form (studying the form)

A horse's 'form' is how it has performed in all its races to date.

In the UK the full form of each racing horse appears in the columns of the sporting press.

At the racecourse on the day a racecard is given to those attending which contains the abbreviated background of each horse.

White Turf Club

This most unusual race meeting is held on the frozen lake in St Moritz, where they have mounted races and ones where the horses tow drivers on skis as well as trotting races where the horses pull an adapted ski-mounted sulky (a light two-wheeled horse-drawn vehicle for one person, used chiefly in harness racing).

Jockey's Colours or Silks

These are the colours the jockeys wear as they race, representing the owner, and were originally made from silk.

The owner of the horse can choose and register their individual racing colour combinations of cap and jersey with Messrs Weatherby, the body responsible for overall administration of horse

racing, for which a fee is paid. If an owner has more than one horse in the same race, the second jockey wears the same jersey but a different coloured silk cap.

Silks were first registered at a meeting in Newmarket in 1762.

Winter Woollies were worn in winter, knitted in wool. But these were found to absorb the damp and sweat which added to the weight whilst racing and are no longer worn!

A Weaver

This is a horse which likes to look over its stable door and appears to rock its head from side to side. Trainers dislike the habit because the head movement is actually caused by the horse moving from one front leg to the other and this can cause problems with the front legs.

This neurotic habit is extremely contagious – if one horse starts it, the others can follow suit.

It can be prevented by putting a weaving bar on the stable door – bars with a V-shaped middle section for the horse to put its head through but which will not allow it to sway.

Weaving is known as a 'vice' and must be declared when selling a horse.

Bumper Race

This is the only Flat race in National Hunt racing, and it is to give young National Hunt horses their early racing experience.

The bumper race is usually the last race of a jumps meeting and is used to ease in prospective jump horses, without them having to handle fences.

Young horses are allowed to run in four or sometimes five bumpers before they go on to hurdles. The distance of a bumper is usually 2 miles although 'junior' bumpers for 3 to 4-year-olds can be run over the shorter distance of 1 mile 4 furlongs.

A Puller (the horse)

A horse that is difficult to hold back and which runs too freely from the start.

The trouble with being a front runner is that the horse can tire or 'fade' before the finish of the race unless the jockey can hold it back until ready to produce its winning run.

A Puller (the jockey)

A jockey who deliberately 'stops' a horse thus preventing it from winning a race. Why might a jockey do that? Well, it could be because he has been paid to do this either by his stable or outside parties.

Whatever the reason, it is highly illegal and any evidence of it will result in a Steward's Enquiry on the course, where they may send it to the BHA Disciplinary Panel. The jockey would be at this stage represented by a solicitor.

First Past the Post

This is the outright winner of the race. The jockey first past the post goes straight to the winner's enclosure where the owners and trainer are gathered. The jockey gives his account of the race to the trainer and owners.

Photographs are taken with the horse and all present. After the jockey has weighed in, he will return to the winners' enclosure where a presentation is made by the sponsors of the race to the owners, trainer, jockey and the lad/lass who looks after the horse and led it up on the day.

The Going

The state of the ground (turf) on the day at a racecourse.

Firm means unyielding, dry ground (you can hear the hooves rattle).

Good is slightly yielding.

Soft means the hooves will make a cut in the ground, and **heavy** is another way of saying muddy.

All-weather artificial turf is always 'standard'.

Every racehorse has its preferred ground, often determined by its breeding.

All-Weather

An artificial racetrack or surface. There are six all-weather tracks at racecourses in the U.K. In the US they are known as 'dirt tracks.'

UK all-weather tracks include Lingfield, Kempton, Southwell, Wolverhampton, Newcastle and Chelmsford. Dundalk is Ireland's all-weather course.

New types of all-weather synthetic tracks are being introduced which allow racing to take place in all weathers when normal turf course racing would not be possible. Racing can also be held under lights for night racing.

• Fibresand is a mixture of various fibres and sand.

• Polytrack is a mixture of silica sand, recycled synthetic fibres (carpet and spondex) and recycled rubber/pvc, the entire mixture coated in wax.

• Tapeta is similar except for the top layer and uses a selection of blended fibres, waxes, pvc and sand up to a depth of 7 inches.

Laytown

Another unusual race meeting,
this one is held once a year on the
first Thursday in September on
the beach at Laytown in Ireland.
The first race was run in 1868.

The tide time-table is rather
important!

It is run under Turf Club rules,
now the Irish Horseracing Board.

Course Doctor

A doctor must attend the whole meeting and tends to any jockeys who may have received injuries during a race. Sometimes their injuries are such that they are sent off to the nearest hospital, and sometimes they are 'stood down' from riding for the rest of the day due to either concussion or minor injuries.

Farrier

Horses' racing shoes are called 'plates'. They are made of a light metal and are put on by a farrier. There is a farrier on the course to replace a shoe if a horse 'has spread a plate'.

Usually if this happens it occurs going down to the start. There will be a short delay whilst the plate is removed and straightened and then put back on.

Plate

This was the monetary winnings for a race, also known as the Purse. The King's Plate was the money the King put up for that particular race.

Most famous Plate races include the Northumberland Plate in the north of England.

Cup

Originally, Cups were races with trophies that had no monetary attachment – you literally just won the cup. Most famous Cups today are the Cheltenham Gold Cup and the huge Foxhunters' Chase Cup.

Whip

The whip carried by a jockey is a regulation size and must comply with the BHA Standard. It is used to stir up a horse and keep him straight. It is not always necessary to use it.

When it is not used (*see* left) this is known as riding the horse with 'hands and heels'. Occasionally the jockey has simply dropped his whip, or does not need to use it. There are one or two races where whips are not allowed at all.

A horse can only be hit on the shoulder or on his quarters behind the saddle. Excessive use of the whip results in a summons to the stewards. A horse may only be hit with a whip 7 times during a Flat race and 8 times in a National Hunt race.

Jockeys who have used up their 'use of the whip' in a race have to resort to pushing out a horse in a tight finish using 'hands and heels' as they wave their whips without touching the horse.

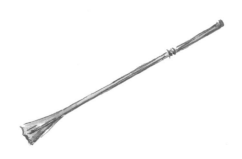

Ringer or Dead Ringer

An identical-looking horse, switched for a faster one as part of a betting scam. Once all-too commonplace, it is nearly impossible to do these days as all racehorses are micro-chipped and must have a passport with which they must travel.

Before they enter the racecourse stables, their passport is checked and the microchip scanned. These passports are held for the duration of the race meeting by the Clerk of the Course. In America racehorses have a lip tattoo with an ID number to prevent the use of Ringers.

National Hunt

or 'Over the Sticks' another term used for races over the jumps, either hurdles or steeple chase fences. National Hunt racing started in Ireland in 1752 and then took off in Britain.

Originally it was a cross country race over fences, ditches, hedges and gates from one church steeple to another, hence the term 'steeplechasing'.

It officially transferred in an organised form on to racecourses in the early 19th century.

In the United States, there are also Timber Races over fixed timber fences: the most famous of which is The Maryland Hunt Cup.

Point-to-Point Races

These are for amateur jockeys only and are usually run by the local hunt. They come under strict BHA regulations.

Point-to-Point races are for horses owned and ridden by members of an affiliated hunt.

The riders must be amateurs (ie. they do not get paid) and the meeting raises much-needed funds for the organising hunt.

Anyone other than a Public Trainer (unless it is his/her own horse) can train a Point-to-Point horse and the only race it can run in, on a National Hunt racecourse, is a Hunter Chase. Point-to-Point horses no longer need to have been hunted to receive a certificate from the Master of Foxhounds.

Nursery Stakes

Nursery handicaps are for two-year-olds only.

By two years old, a thoroughbred will go to a training yard (equine boarding school) to learn how to become a racehorse.

First he will be broken-in, which means he learns to be ridden. He will have fitness training and he will learn to race against others, not least by socialising and running with fellow stable mates.

He will hack out and probably go on the gallops once or twice a week. His trainer will note his progress and assess which races will suit him.

Loose Horse

This is when a horse going down to the start of a race may throw his jockey off and run riderless around the racecourse.

If it is caught and has not travelled too far around the course, it may be allowed to start but if not, the horse is withdrawn.

You occasionally get a horse which escapes from the stalls leaving its rider still in the stalls at the start of a race. What racing commentators call a 'riderless horse' is one which has thrown its jockey during the race.

Walkover

This is when there is only one runner in a race. If all the other entries have been 'scratched', then in order to win by a walkover and collect the prize money, the horse still has to be saddled and paraded and the jockey has to be 'weighed out' in the usual way.

Then the jockey mounts, goes to the start and canters past the stands before once again 'weighing in'.

How to read a Racecard

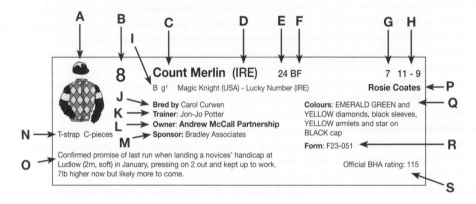

A B C D E F G H

8 Count Merlin (IRE) 24 BF 7 11 - 9

I

B g¹ Magic Knight (USA) - Lucky Number (IRE) Rosie Coates ← P

J

Bred by Carol Curwen

K Trainer: Jon-Jo Potter

L Owner: Andrew McCall Partnership

M Sponsor: Bradley Associates

N → T-strap C-pieces

O

Confirmed promise of last run when landing a novices' handicap at Ludlow (2m, soft) in January, pressing on 2 out and kept up to work. 7lb higher now but likely more to come.

Colours: EMERALD GREEN and YELLOW diamonds, black sleeves, YELLOW armlets and star on BLACK cap ← Q, R

Form: F23-051 ← R

Official BHA rating: 115 ← S

A Owner's silks to be worn by the jockey.

B Number of the horse.

C Racing name of the horse.

D Country of horse's birth.

E Days since horse's last race.

F BF = beaten favourite last time out; D = distance winner to nearest ½ furlong; C = course winner; CD = course and distance winner.

G Age of the horse.

H Weight (lbs/oz) to be carried (stipulated by handicapper)

I Colour (B = bay), sex (g¹ = 1st time gelding).

J Breeder

K Trainer

L Owner

M Sponsor

N T-strap (tongue strap); C-piece (cheek pieces or blinkers)

O Summary of the horse's chances.

P Jockey

Q Colours (silks)

R Form over previous 6 outings. F = fallen; P = pulled up; U = unseated rider; – indicates new year

S Official British Horseracing Authority rating (updated weekly)

Alphabetical Index of Racing Terms

Where a definition is illustrated, we have included the page number.
All other definitions have an explanation only.

Abandoned When bad weather forces the cancellation of a race meeting.

Accumulator A bet in which the winnings from one race automatically go on to your next selected horse.

Amateur jockey 53, 129

Ante-post Better odds are usually offered on bets on horses in major races if placed well in advance.

Apprentice jockey 52

Artificial insemination There is no artificial insemination (A.I.) in thoroughbred racing breeding. If A.I. was allowed it is felt that the gene pool could be flooded with a limited number of genes and that the semen would be cheaper making the stallion's value as a breeding animal much reduced. Not to mention the dodgy dealings of semen not belonging to the stallion at all!

All-weather tracks 113-4

Also-ran 93

Assistant Starter 47-8

Banker 28

Bar 21

Best turned out Racecourse award for the best-groomed horse in the paddock.

Betting slip After you have paid for your bet, you are given a betting slip which gives the details of your wager and which must be presented to the bookie, if you are successful, to claim your winnings.

BHA
The British Horseracing Authority (BHA) is now responsible for the governance, administration and regulation of horse racing and the wider horse racing industry.

Birth date Thoroughbreds are all declared one year old on 1st January regardless of their real date of birth.

Bismarck Horse which bookies expect to lose but punters expect to win.

Blinkers 88

Book-maker / Bookie / Turf accountant 18, 20, 21, 82, 95

Bridles 88

Brood mare 69

Bumper race 105

Byerley Turk First of the three founding sires of all thoroughbred racehorses (b.1680).

Canadian 25

Claiming stakes Races in which all the horses are for sale.

Classics, the 14

Clerk of the Course 62, 125

Colours, horses' 74

Colours, jockey's 100

Colt 63

Combination *see* **Accumulator bet** 24-5

Conditional stakes Races for horses not currently in top ranking.

Course doctor 118

Cup 121

Darley Arabian One of the three founding thoroughbred sires (b. circa 1704).

Doctor, Course 118

Dog A horse that refuses to give its all (or even a little bit) in a race and just doesn't seem to try at all.

Draw 44

Dwells at the start or 'Dwells in the stalls' – phrases for a horse that makes a slow start.

Each-Way bet 30

Facial markings   72
Farrier   119
Favourite Horse with the shortest odds in a race.
Field, the All the horses in a race.
Filly   63
First past the post   110
Fixture A race meeting.
Flat race   58
Foal   70
Forecast Select first and second in a race. A dual forecast is the first two in any order.
Form   96, 136
Front runner Horse that likes to lead from the front all the way.
Furlong An eighth of a mile (220 yards).
Gate   2
Gelding   14
General Stud Book Record of all bloodstock. First published by Weatherbys 1791.
Generous A horse that has the will to win and keeps 'finding more' in a close finish.
Godolphin Arabian One of the three founding thoroughbred sires (b. circa 1724).
Going, the   63, 112
Good trip   14
Gone to post   1
Handicap race is where the horse is given a specific weight to carry which reflects its performance in previous runs. The theory is to give all runners an equal chance of winning.
Hands   78
Hands and heels   122
Hard-ridden When the jockey 'pushes' the horse and uses the whip.
Head Lad   10
Hoods   89
Home straight The straight final stretch of the race track heading to the finish line.
Hurdles Lighter and lower than fences.
In the frame The winning horse, the second and third, their names, number and jockey are put 'in the frame' for all to see.
In the money A horse that finishes in the first 3 (or 4 if a large race).

Jockey Club   54
Jockey's retainer   60
Jockeys   52
Judge   84
Lady jockey   52
Laytown races   116
Legs   77
Length, half length   40-1
Level weights Major race in which all horses carry the same weight.
Loose horse   132
Maiden Stakes   12
Members' Enclosure   94-5
Micro-chip This is inserted into the neck of the horse and contains specific details of the horse. Before the horse can enter the racecourse stables this micro-chip has to be verified. All racing thoroughbreds must be micro-chipped and have an up to date passport (in which its 'flu vaccinations are correctly certified).
Minimum trip The shortest Flat races are five furlongs and two miles over jumps.
Monkey   27
Names of horses Cannot be more than 18 characters and must be registered with Weatherbys.
National Hunt   126
Nod, on the   32
Non-runner Horse that has been withdrawn at the last minute from the race.
Nose, on the   29, 40-1
Noseband   88
Novice race For 2-year-olds which have not won more than twice.
Nursery Stakes   130
Objection Official complaint raised when one horse has impeded another in a race. The owner, trainer or jockey must lodge the objection in writing with the Clerk of the Scales within 5 minutes of the weigh-in.
Odds The ratio paid out by the bookies on the original stake placed.
On the bridle The horse is running well and is moving up through the field.
Off the bridle The horse is not running well and is dropping back through the field.

Off the pace A horse which fails to keep up with the front runners.

On the nod   32

On the nose   29, 40-1

One-paced A horse which does not accelerate.

Outsider Horse unlikely to win and therefore with long odds.

Owners   90

Pacemaker A horse entered in a race by the trainer to ensure the race is run at a fast enough pace to suit his favoured horse.

Paddock / Parade ring   94-5
Where the horses can be viewed for the first time, close-up, by the punters. Owners and trainers are allowed to stand in the centre of the ring, watching their horse going round the paddock and waiting for the jockeys to come out of the Weighing Room. Riding instructions are given to the jockey, he is 'legged up' by the trainer. After another circuit of the paddock the horses are led out to the course and down to the start.

Passport Horse's identifying records which are lodged with the Clerk of the Course before the race.

Permit to train   7

Photo-finish   32

Plate   120

Point-to-Point   129

Pony   26

Pony-ed   34

Post, gone to   1

Pre-Parade Ring On some courses horses may be walked round a pre-parade ring before being taken to the main Parade Ring or Paddock where they can be viewed close-up by the punters.

Professional jockey   46

Pulled up A horse that fails to finish a race.

Puller   106, 108

Punter   18

Pushed on The horse may be dropping out of the race and is urged to go faster.

Racecard, how to read   136

Races (in UK and Ireland) The following are Jockey Club managed racecourses:

Aintree, Carlisle, Cheltenham, Epsom Downs, Exeter, Haydock Park, Huntington, Kempton Park, Market Rasen, Newmarket (the Rowley Mile and the July Course), Nottingham, Sandown Park, Warwick and Wincanton.

Racing Double   22

Rails The white plastic fencing that denotes the track on a racecourse.

Ran on / Full of running When a horse has come from behind in the race and is approaching the leaders but cannot quite catch them. It may be that the race distance has been too short for it.

Riding out a claim The riding out claims are as follows:
In National Hunt racing a Claimer can claim 7lbs off the designated weight for the horse until he/she has won 20 races, 5lbs off until they have won 40 races and 3lbs off until they have won 75 races. (*see* page 46)
Flat Apprentices claim 7lbs off a horses' weight until they have won 20 races; 5lbs until they have won 50 races; and 3lbs until they have won 95 races – after which they have lost their claim and become full professional jockeys.

Rig A male horse whose testicles have not dropped. They have nevertheless been known to father foals.

Right-handed track Here the horses race clockwise; on a left-handed track, they run anti-clockwise.

Ringer   124

Rings   94

Rowley Mile One of two racecourses at Newmarket, named after keen racing fan Charles II.

Runner   82

Saddling Boxes Where the trainer will put saddle and bridle on the horse, usually watched by the owners and other interested parties, after which he enters the Paddock.

Schooling   50

Scratched   38

Selling race The winning horse is put up for auction after the race.